Daddy, Where Are You Now?

Fulton Books
Meadville, PA

Published by Fulton Books 2024

ISBN 979-8-88982-820-4 (paperback)
ISBN 979-8-89221-022-5 (hardcover)
ISBN 979-8-88982-821-1 (digital)

Printed in the United States of America

Daddy, Where Are You Now?

Paul J. Carter

Daddy, where are you now?

I have not gone far.

Sometimes parents grow apart.
It's not your fault.

It's important to know you
will always be loved.

My love for you is like a bright sunny day.
It never diminishes or fades.

I think about you
night and day.

Life has its ups and downs.

I don't want
you to frown.

For you see...

I would drift across many oceans just to hug you.
I would climb the highest mountain just to see you.
I would wander through many lands just to say I love you.

SCHOOL
So for now...
Enjoy being a kid.
Listen to your
mom and dad.
Tell the truth
and never lie.
Never forget
the words "I
love you."
10

As you grow up...
Follow your dreams.
Make the best out of life.
Always believe in yourself and in me.
So ask me how much I love you.
I will tell you, *"A lot."*

A family that stays together is a
family that loves nonstop.

Life goes on, and we must go
where it takes us. But rest
assured I will be there till the end
because my love is forever.

About the Author

Born in 1969, Paul J. Carter is a divorced parent who currently lives in the small state of Delaware. He attended and graduated from Wilmington University with a bachelor's degree in business management with more than twenty-five years of working in the banking industry.